LAUGH
—OUT—
LOUD
Doodles
FOR KIDS

Books by Rob Elliott

LAUGH
—OUT—
LOUD
Doodles

FOR KIDS

ROB ELLIOTT

ILLUSTRATED BY JONNY HAWKINS

Revell

a division of Baker Publishing Group
Grand Rapids, Michigan

Text © 2014 by Rob Elliott
Illustrations © 2014 by Jonny Hawkins

Published by Revell
a division of Baker Publishing Group
P.O. Box 6287, Grand Rapids, MI 49516-6287
www.revellbooks.com

Printed in the United States of America

Library of Congress Cataloging-in-Publication Data is on file at the Library
of Congress, Washington, DC.

ISBN 978-0-8007-2446-7

14   15   16   17   18   19   20   7   6   5   4   3

The LAUGH-OUT-LOUD HUMOR CODE
by Rob Elliott

1. Don't make jokes at other people's expense.

2. Keep it clean.

3. Laughter is great medicine so find something to laugh at every day.

4. Tell your favorite jokes to as many people as you can to brighten up their days, too!

5. Body noise and body fluid jokes are the best.

urp

'scuse me... hee hee.

94

MY CODE OF HUMOR

1.

2.

3.

4.

5.

Write and doodle your own humor code.

Doodle yourself telling your favorite joke.

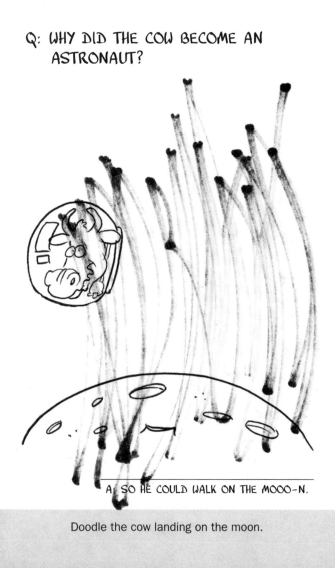

Q: WHY DID THE COW BECOME AN ASTRONAUT?

A: SO HE COULD WALK ON THE MOOO-N.

Doodle the cow landing on the moon.

Q: WHERE DO PIGS GO FOR A REST?

A: TO THEIR HAM-MOCK.

Doodle the pig's resting place and surroundings.

Q: HOW DOES AN ESKIMO FIX HIS
   BROKEN TOY?

A: WITH IGLOO.

Finish doodling the joke.

Q: WHAT KIND OF TEETH COST MONEY?

A: BUCK TEETH.

Doodle the joke.

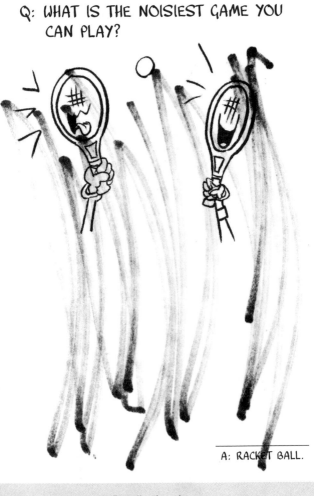

Doodle the players.

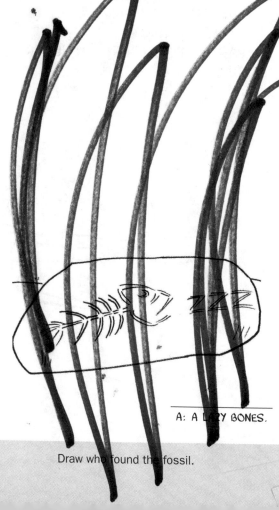

Q: WHAT DO YOU CALL A FOSSIL THAT NEVER DOES ANY WORK?

A: A LAZY BONES.

Draw who found the fossil.

KNOCK KNOCK.
  WHO'S THERE?
PASTOR.
  PASTOR WHO?
PASTOR POTATOES, I'M HUNGRY.

Draw the scene around the table.

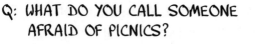

Q: WHAT DO YOU CALL SOMEONE AFRAID OF PICNICS?

A: A BASKET CASE.

Draw the people, what they're eating,
and what they're afraid of.

Q: WHAT DID THE MOTHER LION SAY TO HER CUBS BEFORE DINNER?

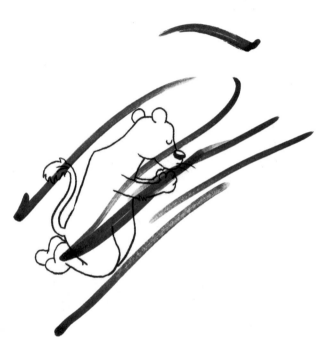

A: SHALL WE PREY?

Draw the cubs and what they're eating.

Q: HOW DID THE FRENCH FRY PROPOSE
   TO THE HAMBURGER?

A: HE GAVE HER AN ONION RING.

Finish lady burger. Who else is here?

Q: WHY ARE FISH SO BAD AT BASKETBALL?

A: THEY DON'T LIKE GETTING CLOSE TO THE NET.

Doodle the scared fish with the ball.

KNOCK KNOCK.
  WHO'S THERE?
CANOE.
  CANOE WHO?
CANOE COME OUT AND PLAY?

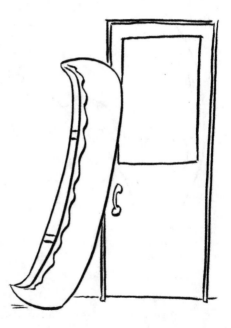

Whose canoe? Who's in the window?

Q: WHAT DID THE WHALE SAY TO THE DOLPHIN?

A: LONG TIME, NO SEA.

Finish doodling the bodies and
the other life in the sea.

Q: WHAT DO YOU CALL A MONKEY THAT
   WON'T BEHAVE?

A: A BAD-BOON.

What mess has the monkey made?

Q: WHAT DO YOU CALL A COW THAT CAN'T GIVE MILK?

A: A MILK DUD.

Draw the rest of the cow, the bucket, and the farmer.

KNOCK KNOCK.
WHO'S THERE?
EILEEN.
EILEEN WHO?
I'M SO TALL, EILEEN OVER TO
GET THROUGH THE DOOR!

Draw tall Eileen in the doorway.

KNOCK KNOCK.
WHO'S THERE?
SHELBY.
SHELBY WHO?
SHELBY COMING 'ROUND THE
MOUNTAIN WHEN SHE COMES!

Doodle her coming 'round the mountain!

Q: WHY COULDN'T THE MONSTER GO TO SLEEP?

A: IT WAS AFRAID THERE WERE KIDS UNDER THE BED!

Draw the poor frightened monster.

Q: WHAT'S A WHALE'S FAVORITE GAME?

A: SWALLOW THE LEADER.

Draw a whale of a meal.

Q: WHAT DO YOU GET WHEN YOUR DOG MAKES YOU BREAKFAST?

A: POOCHED EGGS.

Finish the dog's egg-splosive creation.

KNOCK KNOCK.
  WHO'S THERE?
WOODY.
  WOODY WHO?
WOODY LIKE TO HEAR ANOTHER
  KNOCK-KNOCK JOKE?

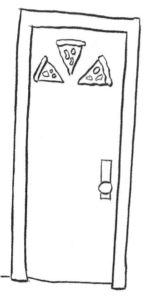

Doodle it!

KNOCK KNOCK.
  WHO'S THERE?
DUNCAN.
  DUNCAN WHO?
DUNCAN COOKIES IN
  MILK TASTES GOOD.

Draw the dunk divers.

Q: WHAT DID THE WOLF DO WHEN HE HEARD THE JOKE?

A: HE HOWLED.

Doodle a howling wolf or two-oo-oo!

Q: WHAT HAPPENED TO THE BEANS
   WHEN THEY SHOWED UP LATE TO
   WORK?

Bean Factory

A: THEY GOT CANNED.

Who's the boss? Draw the factory.

Draw your favorite humor companions.

KNOCK KNOCK.
  WHO'S THERE?
ROCKEFELLER.
  ROCKEFELLER WHO?
ROCKEFELLER IN HIS CRADLE AND
  HE'LL GO RIGHT TO SLEEP.

Draw who's in the cradle . . . and who is rocking it.

Q: HOW DID THE KARATE TEACHER GREET HIS STUDENTS?

A: "HI-YAH!"

Finish doodling the karate teacher and his students.

Q: WHAT KIND OF LIGHTS DID NOAH USE ON THE ARK?

A: FLOOD LIGHTS.

Doodle the rest of the ark, the animals, and the lighting.

A: JELLY FISH.

Where's the peanut butter and the other nutty fish?

Q: WHAT'S YOUR FAVORITE HOBBY?

Doodle your hobby and write a joke to go with it!

Q: WHY DID THE CAT GET DETENTION AT SCHOOL?

A: BECAUSE HE WAS A CHEETAH.

Finish the little cheetah and his schoolroom.

Q: HOW DID THOMAS EDISON INVENT
   THE LIGHTBULB?

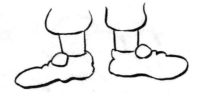

A: HE GOT A BRIGHT IDEA!

Finish Mr. Edison and his bright idea.

Q: WHY DID THE ROBBER WASH HIS CLOTHES BEFORE HE RAN AWAY WITH THE LOOT?

A: HE WANTED TO MAKE A CLEAN GETAWAY.

Draw the robber and his getaway.

Q: WHAT SOUND DO PORCUPINES MAKE WHEN THEY KISS?

A: OUCH! OUCH!

Draw the other painful kissing porcupine.

Q: WHAT IS A WHALE'S FAVORITE CANDY?

A: BLUBBER GUM.

Draw the whale's favorite candy and yours too!

TONGUE TWISTER:
SAY IT 10 TIMES FAST . . .
FRESH FRENCH FRIES.

Doodle the ketchup and saltshaker.

KNOCK KNOCK.
   WHO'S THERE?
BACON.
   BACON WHO?
I'M BACON A CAKE FOR
   YOUR BIRTHDAY.

Draw the cake, the baker, and the party!

Q: WHAT DO YOU GET IF YOU MIX A RABBIT AND A SNAKE?

A: A JUMP ROPE.

Finish doodling the joke.

Q: WHY DID THE ROOSTER GO TO THE DOCTOR?

A: IT HAD THE COCK-A-DOODLE FLU.

Draw the sick rooster, the nurse, and anyone with him.

Q: WHAT DO YOU CALL AN INSECT THAT COMPLAINS ALL THE TIME?

A: A GRUMBLE BEE.

Doodle the grumbling insect.
What lies and flies beneath?

Q: WHAT WOULD YOU GET IF YOU THREW ALL THE BOOKS IN THE OCEAN?

A: A TITLE WAVE.

Draw the covers of your favorite books.

KNOCK KNOCK.
 WHO'S THERE?
WAYNE.
 WAYNE WHO?
THE WAYNE IS REALLY COMING DOWN
 . . . SO OPEN THE DOOR!

Finish the joke!

Q: WHAT IS A SHEEP'S FAVORITE KIND OF FOOD?

A: BAA-BAA-CUE.

What is the sheep grilling?
What's on the sheep's apron?

Q: WHY DID THE SKUNK HAVE TO STAY IN BED UNTIL IT FELT BETTER?

A: IT WAS THE DOCTOR'S ODORS.

Doodle the doc and anything else in the room.

Q: WHAT IS THE BEST FOOD TO EAT WHEN YOU'RE SCARED?

A: I SCREAM!

Doodle it!

Q: WHAT WAS THE BEST TIME OF DAY
   IN THE MIDDLE AGES?

A: KNIGHT-TIME.

Draw the suit of armor and the
horse and finish the castle.

Q: WHAT DO YOU CALL A PIG THAT IS NO FUN TO BE AROUND?

A: A BOAR.

Take your pig pen and doodle the boar-ing pig.

Who's knocking on the door?

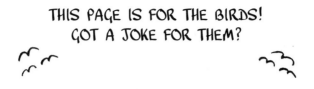

THIS PAGE IS FOR THE BIRDS!
GOT A JOKE FOR THEM?

Riddle and doodle it yourself.

Q: WHY DID THE BANANA WEAR
SUNSCREEN AT THE BEACH?

A: IT DIDN'T WANT TO PEEL.

Finish doodling the banana on the beach.

TONGUE TWISTER:
SAY IT 10 TIMES FAST . . .
SOCK, SKIRT, SHIRT.

Doodle the twister!

A: A PENGUIN THAT'S EMBARRASSED.

Pen the penguin's expression.

Q: WHAT IS A REPTILE'S FAVORITE MOVIE?

A: *THE LIZARD OF OZ!*

Draw what the lizard is watching.

Q: WHAT DO COWS LIKE TO EAT?

A: SMOOTHIES.

Finish drawing the cows and their drinks.

Q: IF APRIL SHOWERS BRING
MAY FLOWERS, WHAT DO
MAY FLOWERS BRING?

A: PILGRIMS.

Doodle the rest of the joke.

KNOCK KNOCK.
  WHO'S THERE?
LES.
  LES WHO?
LES CUT THE SMALL
  TALK AND LET ME IN!

Draw what Les is saying and who he's talking to.

KNOCK KNOCK.
 WHO'S THERE?
WADDLE.
 WADDLE WHO?
WADDLE YOU DO IF I TELL ANOTHER
 KNOCK-KNOCK JOKE?

Finish the waddler and doodle a friend or two.

Q: WHAT DO POTATOES WEAR TO BED?

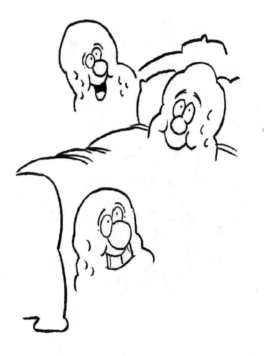

A: YAMMIES.

Finish the taters in their nightclothes.

Q: WHY WOULDN'T THE TEAM PLAY WITH
   THE THIRD BASKETBALL?

A: BECAUSE IT WAS AN ODDBALL.

Doodle a third player and the joke!

Q: WHAT DO YOU GET WHEN YOU THROW A PIG INTO THE BUSHES?

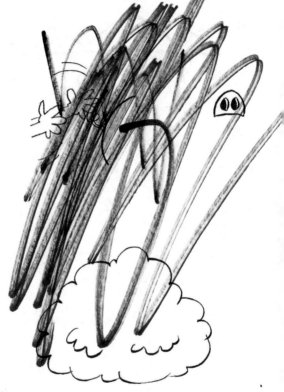

A: A HEDGEHOG.

Draw the flying pig and his surprised expression. Where will he land?

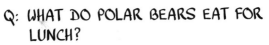

Q: WHAT DO POLAR BEARS EAT FOR LUNCH?

A: ICEBERG-ERS!

Doodle the bear and its meal.

KNOCK KNOCK.
 WHO'S THERE?
LITTLE OLD LADY.
 LITTLE OLD LADY WHO?
I DIDN'T KNOW YOU COULD YODEL!

Finish the little old lady and draw a yodeler.

A: CHEESE AND QUACKERS.

Doodle the duck's snacks.

Draw what the weasel is saying and who
he's talking to through the window.

A: ROCK 'N' ROLL.

Finish drawing the rock, the
instruments, and the band.

Q: HOW ARE A MOUSE AND A WHEEL ALIKE?

A: THEY BOTH SQUEAK.

Finish the mouse. What's on the cart?

Q: WHY DID THE TREES TAKE A NAP?

A: FOR REST!

Draw the rest of the forest resting.

Q: WHAT'S YOUR DAD'S FAVORITE JOKE?

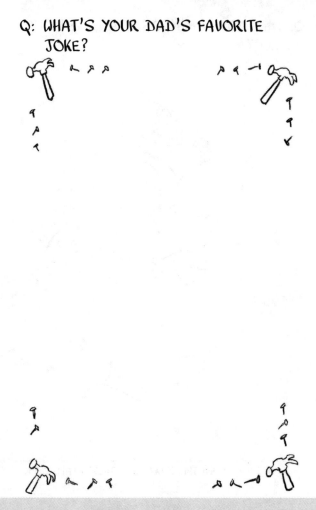

Write and doodle Dad's joke!

Q: WHY DO FLAMINGOS STAND ON ONE
   LEG?

A: IF THEY LIFTED THE OTHER LEG, THEY'D FALL OVER.

Finish the flamingo and its pond.

Q: WHAT IS A HYENA'S FAVORITE KIND OF CANDY?

A: A SNICKERS BAR.

Doodle the hyena's funny food.

Q: WHERE DO LUMBERJACKS KEEP THEIR PIGS?

A: IN THEIR HOG CABIN.

Finish doodling the joke!

Q: WHAT RUNS AROUND THE FOOTBALL FIELD BUT NEVER MOVES?

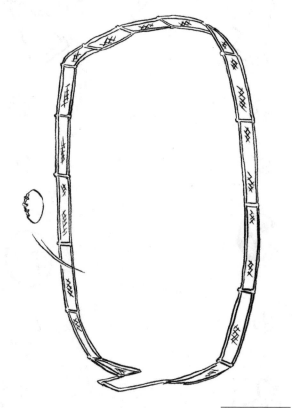

A: A FENCE.

Flip to the right and doodle a field
and a player or two . . .

Q: WHAT IS YOUR FAVORITE SPORT?

Be a good sport and draw it!
And write a winning joke to go with it!

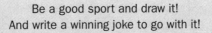

Q: WHY DID SALLY'S COMPUTER KEEP SNEEZING?

GESUNDHEIT!

A: IT HAD A VIRUS.

Draw the tech trouble . . . what a mess!

KNOCK KNOCK.
  WHO'S THERE?
BUTTER.
  BUTTER WHO?
I BUTTER NOT TELL YOU—
  IT'S A SECRET.

You butter finish drawing the joke.

Q: WHAT DID THE HORSE SAY WHEN HE TRIPPED?

A: HELP! I'VE FALLEN AND I CAN'T GIDDY-UP.

Doodle what the horse is saying
and what he tripped over.

Q: WHY DO RHINOS HAVE SO MANY WRINKLES?

A: BECAUSE THEY'RE SO HARD TO IRON.

Draw the rest of the wrinkly rhino . . .
maybe a bird on his back?

TONGUE TWISTER:
SAY IT 10 TIMES FAST . . .
TALL TREES TOSS LEAVES.

Finish the top of the tree.

Q: WHY DO SEAGULLS FLY OVER THE SEA?

A: BECAUSE IF THEY FLEW OVER THE BAY, THEY'D BE BAGELS.

Doodle the joke!

Q: WHAT LANGUAGE DOES A BILLBOARD SPEAK?

A: SIGN LANGUAGE.

What's on this sign?

A: THEY DON'T LIKE BATS!

Draw the joke.

TONGUE TWISTER:
SAY IT 10 TIMES FAST . . .
SELFISH SHELLFISH.

What's in the treasure chest?
Doodle the other life in the sea.

Q: WHY COULDN'T THE GOATS GET ALONG?

A: THEY KEPT BUTTING HEADS.

Who is he charging?

Q: WHAT DO YOU CALL A BEAR STANDING IN THE RAIN?

A: DRIZZLY BEAR.

Finish doodling the bear in the rain.

Q: WHAT IS THE CHEAPEST WAY TO
TRAVEL?

A: BY SALE-BOAT!

Doodle it!

A: BECAUSE THEY'RE ALWAYS PEAKING.

What is the mountain peaking at?
Draw the faces and places too!

TONGUE TWISTER:
SAY IT 10 TIMES FAST . . .
SIX SLIMY SNAILS SAILED SILENTLY.

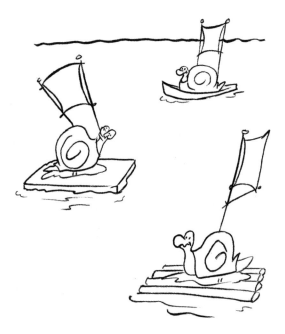

Draw the missing snails and sails!

Q: WHY WOULDN'T THE LION EAT THE CLOWN?

A: HE TASTED FUNNY!

Start clowning around . . . doodle the joke!

Q: EVER HAD A MENTAL BLOCK?

We did! Write your own joke . . . and doodle it too!

Q: WHAT IS A WOODPECKER'S FAVORITE JOKE?

A: A KNOCK-KNOCK JOKE.

Finish the tree, the sky above him,
and the ground below him.

Q: WHY DID BILLY HAVE A HOT DOG IN HIS SHOE?

A: IT WAS A FOOT-LONG!

Draw the joke . . . supersize it!

Q: WHAT KIND OF BIRD LIKES TO MAKE BREAD?

A: THE DODO BIRD.

Finish the bird and decorate her kitchen.

Q: WHY COULDN'T THE ELEPHANTS GO SWIMMING AT THE POOL?

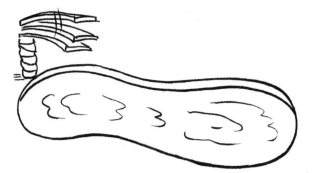

A: THEY WERE ALWAYS LOSING THEIR TRUNKS.

Finish the animals and what's around the pool.

KNOCK KNOCK.
   WHO'S THERE?
OLIVE.
   OLIVE WHO?
OLIVE YOU! DO YOU LOVE ME TOO?

Finish drawing Olive and the one she loves.

Q: WHY DID JIMMY'S PARENTS SCREAM WHEN THEY SAW HIS GRADES?

A: BECAUSE HE HAD A BEE ON HIS REPORT CARD!

Doodle Jimmy, his parents, and
anything else you think of.

TONGUE TWISTER:
SAY IT 10 TIMES FAST . . .
SNEAKY SNAKES SLITHER SLOWLY.

Where are the other hiss-ss-ss-ing creepy crawlers?

KNOCK KNOCK.
  WHO'S THERE?
NOSE.
  NOSE WHO?
I NOSE A LOT MORE KNOCK-KNOCK
  JOKES IF YOU WANT TO HEAR THEM.

Who is attached to the nose?

Q: DID YOU KNOW THAT A KANGAROO CAN JUMP HIGHER THAN YOUR HOUSE?

A: OF COURSE! YOUR HOUSE CAN'T JUMP!

Finish the kangaroo and doodle funny clouds.

Q: HOW DID BENJAMIN FRANKLIN FEEL ABOUT DISCOUERING ELECTRICITY?

A: HE WAS SHOCKED!

Complete Ben, his kite, and the whole electrifying experience.

Q: CAN YOU THINK OF A JOKE INVOLVING A ROCK?

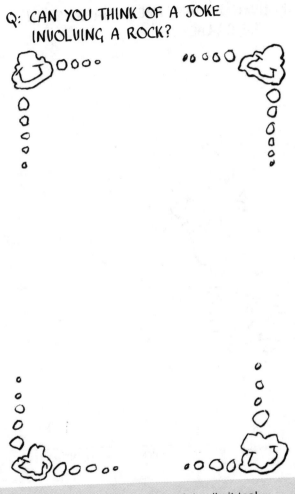

Rock on! Write the joke and doodle it too!

Q: WHEN DO YOU NEED CHAPSTICK IN THE GARDEN?

A: WHEN YOU'RE PLANTING TULIPS.

Finish the gardener and the garden too.

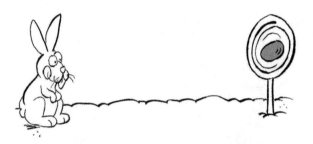

A: JELLY BEANS.

But what if they did? Doodle the jelly bean garden.

Q: WHY WERE THE DEER, THE CHIPMUNK, AND THE SQUIRREL LAUGHING SO HARD?

A: BECAUSE THE OWL WAS A HOOT!

Draw the wise guy.

Q: WHAT DO YOU GET IF A COW IS IN AN EARTHQUAKE?

A: A MILKSHAKE.

Finish the quaking cow and the rest of the joke.

Q: WHY DID THE GOLFER WEAR TWO
PAIRS OF PANTS?

A: IN CASE HE GOT A HOLE IN ONE.

Finish drawing the joke!

Q: WHY DID THE LETTUCE WIN THE RACE?

A: HE WAS A HEAD.

Draw the other veggie runners in the race.

Q: WHERE IS A PLACE YOU'VE ALWAYS WANTED TO GO?

Draw it! And write a joke to travel with it . . .

Q: WHY WAS THE INCREDIBLE HULK SO GOOD WITH PLANTS?

A: HE HAD A GREEN THUMB.

Doodle the kind of plant Hulk would grow.
You can even draw Hulk, if you dare!

Q: WHY DID THE MAN PUT HIS MONEY IN THE FREEZER?

A: HE WANTED SOME COLD, HARD CASH!

Draw the joke. Decorate the fridge.

Q: WHAT HAPPENS WHEN YOU PHONE A CLOWN THREE TIMES?

A: YOU HAVE A THREE-RING CIRCUS.

Doodle the frazzled and funny clown.

Q: HOW DO YOU GREET A FROG?

A: "WART'S UP?"

Doodle the frog's friend and the rest of the joke.

A: ITS FAIRY COD-MOTHER.

Doodle the one with the wand.

Q: WHY WERE THE ROBINS EATING CAKE?

A: BECAUSE IT WAS THEIR BIRD-THDAY.

Decorate the cake and room for the party.

Is Hannah a horse? Of course! Draw her!

Q: WHAT IS A POLAR BEAR'S FAVORITE BREAKFAST?

A: ICE KRISPIES.

Design the cereal box.

Q: WHY WAS THE FROG IN A BAD MOOD?

A: BECAUSE HE WAS HAVING A TOAD-ALLY BAD DAY.

Express yourself! Fill in the froggy's face.

Q: WHAT IS AN ALIEN'S FAVORITE KIND OF CANDY?

A: A MARS BAR.

Draw the out-of-this-world treat!

TONGUE TWISTER:
SAY IT 10 TIMES FAST . . .
BEEFY BLAZING BISON BURGERS.

Doodle who's enjoying the burger!

A: I'M ROOTING FOR YOU!

Finish the joke and what the tree
is saying to the flower.

KNOCK KNOCK.
  WHO'S THERE?
JOANNA.
  JOANNA WHO?
JOANNA COME OUT AND PLAY?

Draw Joanna at the door.

Q: WHERE DO OLD ANTS GO?

A: THE ANT-IQUE STORE.

Doodle the storefront!

A: YOU LOOK LIKE A FUNGI!

Draw the joke. What is the tomato saying?

Q: WHERE DO YOU KEEP YOUR JOKES?

A: IN A GIGGLE BOX.

Finish the joke!

KNOCK KNOCK.
WHO'S THERE?
CARSON.
CARSON WHO?
CARSON THE FREEWAY
DRIVE REALLY FAST!

Draw the fast car and anything else
you think is on the freeway.

Q: HOW DID THE PIG WRITE A LETTER?

A: WITH ITS PIG PEN.

Finish the pig and draw a fun hat on him too!

Q: WHAT DID THE NIGHT CRAWLER'S PARENTS SAY WHEN THEIR CHILD GOT HOME AFTER CURFEW?

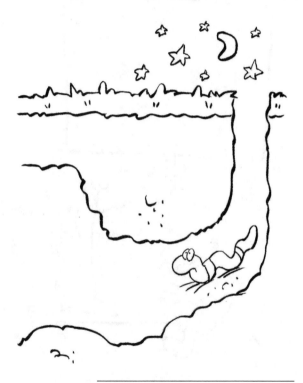

A: WHERE ON EARTH HAVE YOU BEEN?

Doodle that "not too happy" mom and dad!

Q: WHAT IS A DOG'S MOTTO?

A: DON'T BARK UP THE WRONG TREE.

Finish the dog. Write out his motto
or come up with a new one.

Q: WHY DID THE COMPUTER GET
   GLASSES?

A: TO IMPROVE HIS WEBSITE.

Doodle the glasses and any other
features you think of!

Q: DO YOU HAVE A JOKE TO GO WITH THIS?

Write and doodle it!

Q: WHEN DO YOU STOP AT GREEN AND
GO ON RED?

A: WHEN YOU'RE EATING A WATERMELON.

Who's eating it?

Q: WHERE IS THE BEST PLACE TO PARK
YOUR DOG?

A: THE BARKING LOT.

Doodle the doggy.

Q: WHAT DO YOU GET WHEN YOU CROSS A RABBIT AND A FROG?

A: A BUNNY RIBBIT.

Hop to it! What would that look like?

Q: HOW DO CHICKENS STAY IN SHAPE?

A: THEY EGGS-ERCISE.

Doodle the other buff chickens.

KNOCK KNOCK.
  WHO'S THERE?
ARCHIE.
  ARCHIE WHO?
ARCHIE GOING TO LET ME IN?

Draw Archie and the rest of the picture.

Q: WHY WAS THE CHEETAH WEARING
   GLASSES?

A: HE WAS SEEING SPOTS.

Finish its face . . . with specs.

A: A TEDDY BOAR.

Finish the beast!

Q: WHERE DO BUGS GO SHOPPING?

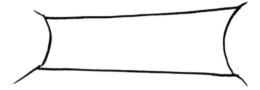

A: THE FLEA MARKET.

Draw the joke with the buyers and sellers.

Q: DID YOU HEAR ABOUT THE ACTOR WHO FELL THROUGH THE FLOOR?

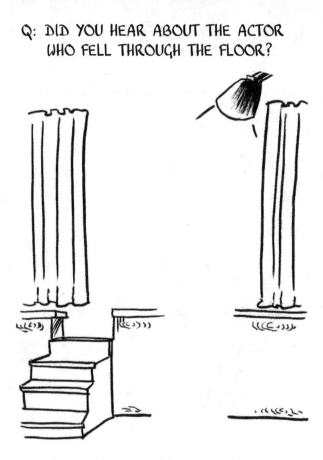

A: IT WAS JUST A STAGE HE WAS GOING THROUGH.

Draw the joke. Give it a cr-r-rack!

Q: WHAT DO ELVES LEARN IN KINDERGARTEN?

A: THE ELF-ABET.

What's on the board?

Q: WHY DID THE MONKEY ALMOST GET FIRED?

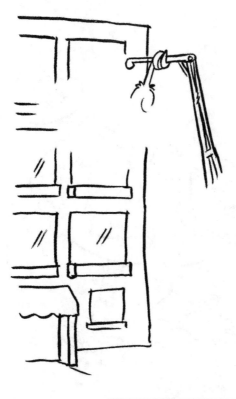

A: IT TOOK HIM AWHILE TO GET INTO THE SWING OF THINGS.

Doodle the window-washing monkey
. . . and finish the crane.

Finish the brilliant being.

Draw the joke.

Q: WHAT HAPPENED WHEN THE GIRAFFES
   HAD A RACE?

A: THEY WERE NECK AND NECK THE WHOLE TIME.

Doodle the other racer.

Q: HOW DO YOU MAKE A HOT DOG STAND?

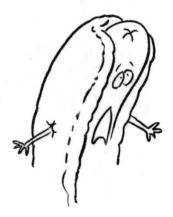

A: TAKE AWAY ITS CHAIR.

Finish the hot dog. Where is the chair,
and did someone pull it away?

Q: WHAT DO YOU CALL A CAT WITH
EIGHT LEGS THAT CAN SWIM?

A: OCTO-PUSS.

Draw the joke and a sea of catfish!

A: THE PRAWN SHOP.

Draw the joke.

Q: WHO EARNS A LIVING DRIVING THEIR CUSTOMERS AWAY?

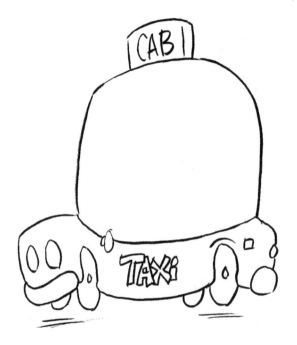

A: TAXI DRIVERS.

Who's driving? Who's riding? Draw the car-toon.

Q: WHY WAS THE BASEBALL PLAYER A
   BAD SPORT?

A: HE STOLE THIRD BASE AND WENT HOME.

Finish the bandit, the field, and other players.

Q: WHAT IS GREEN AND CAN SING?

A: ELVIS PARSLEY.

Draw the joke.

KNOCK KNOCK.
 WHO'S THERE?
OTTER.
 OTTER WHO?
YOU OTTER OPEN THIS DOOR
 AND LET ME IN!

Who's at the door?

Q: WHAT DO YOU GET WHEN YOU CROSS A BEAR WITH A FOREST?

A: YOU GET FUR TREES.

Finish doodling the joke.

A: THE SOAP-RANOS.

Finish drawing the choir. What are they singing?

Q: WHAT IS THE DIFFERENCE BETWEEN A FOOTBALL PLAYER AND A DOG?

A: A FOOTBALL PLAYER HAS A WHOLE UNIFORM, BUT A DOG ONLY PANTS.

Decorate the helmet and uniform. Where's the dog?

Q: DID YOU HEAR ABOUT THE TEACHER WHO WAS CROSS-EYED?

A: SHE COULDN'T CONTROL HER PUPILS.

Face up to the joke and finish the teacher.

KNOCK KNOCK.
   WHO'S THERE?
DRAGON.
   DRAGON WHO?
QUIT DRAGON THIS OUT
   AND OPEN THE DOOR!

Who's in that door window? A knight?

Q: WHAT DO YOU GET WHEN YOU HAVE TWO DOCTORS AT ONCE?

A: PAIR-A-MEDICS.

Finish the healthy humor.

Q: WHAT IS THE DIFFERENCE BETWEEN BOOGERS AND BROCCOLI?

A: KIDS WON'T EAT THEIR BROCCOLI.

Draw the joke! Ga-rosss!

Q: WHAT WAS THE MATH TEACHER'S FAVORITE DESSERT?

A: Pi.

What's on the board? Finish the teacher!

Q: WHAT KIND OF BIRD IS ALWAYS DEPRESSED?

A: A BLUEBIRD.

Doodle some birds that can cheer poor bluebird up.

Q: WHAT DO YOU GET WHEN YOU PUT
   GLASSES ON A PONY?

A: A SEE-HORSE.

I see you need to finish the joke. No horsing around!

Q: WHERE SHOULD A 600-POUND LION GO?

A: ON A DIET!

Finish the fat cat. Add some yummy snacks too.

Who's holding the dishes?

WHAT'S YOUR MOM'S FAVORITE JOKE?

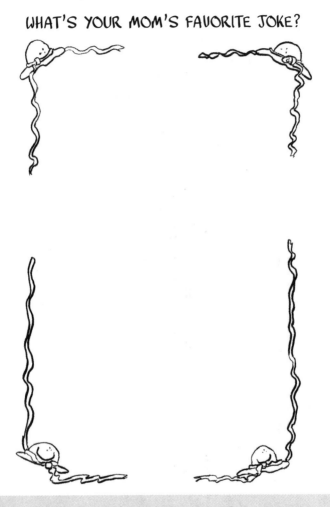

Write the joke and doodle the mother of all crack-ups!

Q: HOW DOES A GINGERBREAD MAN
MAKE HIS BED?

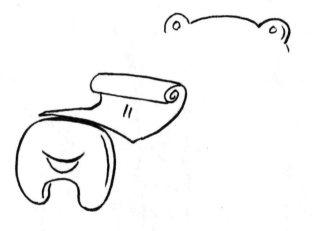

A: WITH A COOKIE SHEET.

Draw the gingerbread man and bring his room to life.

Q: WHY WAS EVERYONE LOOKING UP TO THE CEILING AND CHEERING?

A: THEY WERE CEILING FANS!

Doodle others cheering (dogs and cats too)!

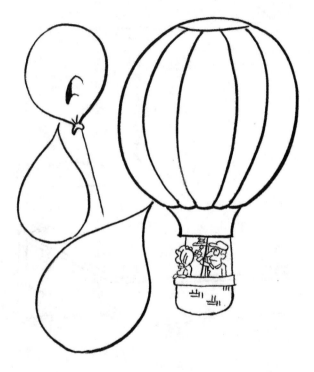

Q: WHY CAN'T YOU TAKE ANYTHING BALLOONS SAY SERIOUSLY?

A: THEY'RE ALWAYS FULL OF HOT AIR.

Say! . . . What are the balloons saying?

A: IN THEIR WATERBEDS.

Draw sleeping fish and any other
sea creatures you'd like.

Q: WHAT WILL A MOOSE DO IF HE CALLS WHEN YOU'RE NOT HOME?

A: HE'LL LEAVE A DETAILED MOOSE-AGE.

What is he saying?

A: DROP IT A LINE!

Draw the fisherman and the fish too!

KNOCK KNOCK.
  WHO'S THERE?
OWL.
  OWL WHO?
OWL TELL YOU ANOTHER JOKE
  IF YOU LET ME IN.

Finish the door and the person on the other side.

Q: WHY WAS THE NOSE FEELING SAD?

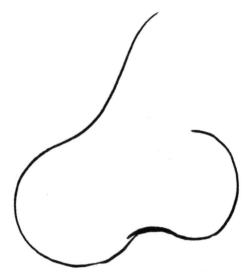

A: IT WAS TIRED OF GETTING PICKED ON.

What creative or crazy ideas can
you doodle? Who nose?

Q: WHAT DID THE ICE CREAM RIDE TO THE STORE?

A: A FUDGE-CYCLE.

Finish doodling this tasteful joke!

Q: WHAT DO YOU CALL A MAN WITH A SEAGULL ON HIS HEAD?

A: CLIFF.

Doodle the seagull . . . make it large and loony!

Q: WHAT'S MORE ANNOYING THAN A CAT MEOWING OUTSIDE YOUR BEDROOM WINDOW?

A: TEN CATS MEOWING OUTSIDE YOUR BEDROOM WINDOW.

Finish the joke!

Q: WHY ARE PIGS SO BAD AT FOOTBALL?

A: THEY'RE ALWAYS HOGGING THE BALL.

Finish the pig.

Q: WHY DID THE COWBOY GO OUT AND
   BUY A WIENER DOG?

A: BECAUSE SOMEONE TOLD HIM TO
   "GET A LONG, LITTLE DOGGIE."

Finish the cowboy and his dog.

Q: WHAT HAPPENS WHEN YOU GET A
THOUSAND BUNNIES TO LINE UP
AND JUMP BACKWARD?

A: YOU HAVE A RECEDING HARE LINE.

Draw 997 other jumping bunnies.

Q: WHAT DID THE TREE SAY TO THE LUMBERJACK?

A: LEAF ME ALONE!

Doodle the talking treetop.

Q: WHAT DID THE EARTHQUAKE SAY TO
   THE TORNADO?

A: DON'T LOOK AT ME. IT'S NOT MY FAULT!

Draw a tornado. Give it a whirl!

KNOCK KNOCK.
  WHO'S THERE?
ADA.
  ADA WHO?
ADA LOT OF SWEETS AND
  NOW I FEEL SICK.

Where's Ada?

KNOCK KNOCK.
  WHO'S THERE?
LUCAS.
  LUCAS WHO?
LUCAS IN THE EYE AND TELL US
  YOU DON'T WANT TO HEAR
  ANOTHER KNOCK-KNOCK JOKE!

Who is Lucas looking in the eye?

Q: WHAT IS A PIG'S FAVORITE PLAY?

A: HAMLET.

Fill the muddy stage.

TONGUE TWISTER:
SAY IT 10 TIMES FAST . . .
PURPLE PENGUINS PLAY PING-PONG.

Where is the other penguin?
Can you make them purple?

Q: WHERE DO SKUNKS LIKE TO SIT IN CHURCH?

A: IN THE FRONT PEW.

Who is sitting next to stinky?

Q: WHAT DOES A FROG DRINK WHEN IT
   WANTS TO LOSE WEIGHT?

A: DIET CROAK.

Doodle froggy getting a drink.
Can you think of other silly soda titles?

KNOCK KNOCK.
  WHO'S THERE?
AMOS.
  AMOS WHO?
OUCH! AMOS-QUITO BIT ME!

Doodle who got it! Itchy!

Q: WHY DIDN'T THE LLAMA GET ANY DESSERT?

A: HE WOULDN'T EAT ANY OF HIS LLAMA BEANS.

Finish doodling the joke! What's on the llama's plate? On the table?

Q: WHY DID THE PONY GET SENT TO HIS ROOM WITHOUT SUPPER?

A: HE WOULDN'T STOP HORSIN' AROUND.

Finish pony's messy room.

Q: WHEN DO PINE TREES LIKE TO DO EMBROIDERY?

A: WHEN THEY DO NEEDLEPOINT.

Doodle the tree-mendously sharp creations on the wall!

Q: HOW DOES A FARMER COUNT HIS CATTLE?

A: WITH A COW-CULATOR.

Cow-nting on you to moo-oove your
pencil and add cows.

Q: WHY IS IT SO EASY FOR AN
ELEPHANT TO GET A JOB?

A: BECAUSE IT WILL WORK FOR PEANUTS.

Finish the elephant. What's his job?

KNOCK KNOCK.
  WHO'S THERE?
COOK.
  COOK WHO?
ARE YOU AS CRAZY AS YOU SOUND?

Draw the crazy one the cook is meeting.

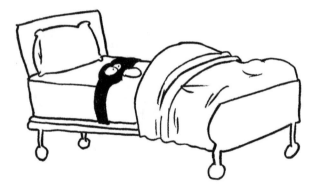

A: IT WAS UNDERCOVER.

Doodle someone jumping on the bed.

Q: WHAT IS THE BEST KIND OF CAT TO HAVE AROUND?

A: A DANDY-LION.

Doodle the joke. Can you add more around him?

Q: WHY DID THE CHICKENS GET IN
TROUBLE AT SCHOOL?

A: THEY WERE USING FOWL LANGUAGE.

Where is the teacher? Fill in the classroom.

Q: WHAT DID THE FROGS SAY TO EACH OTHER ON THEIR WEDDING DAY?

A: I'LL LOVE YOU UNTIL THE DAY I CROAK.

Doodle the froggy's bride and the pastor/priest.

Doodle it from an air guitar to a "there" guitar. Make notes too!

A: BY LOCO-MOTIVE.

Finish the joke. Who's driving this insane train?

Q: WHAT DO YOU GIVE A PIG THAT HAS A COLD?

A: TROUGH SYRUP.

Draw the joke. Doodle yourself pouring.

Q: WHICH CREATURES IN NOAH'S ARK DIDN'T COME IN PAIRS?

A: THE WORMS—THEY CAME IN APPLES.

Where are those wiggly ones? Other critters?

Q: WHAT DID THE PAPER SAY TO THE PENCIL?

A: YOU'VE GOT A GOOD POINT!

Get the lead (or graphite) out and doodle a pencil!

KNOCK KNOCK.
  WHO'S THERE?
AARDVARK.
  AARDVARK WHO?
AARDVARK A THOUSAND MILES
  JUST TO SEE YOU!

Doodle who is at the door window. Ants? Uncles?

Q: WHY WOULDN'T THE TEDDY BEAR
EAT ANYTHING?

A: HE WAS ALREADY STUFFED.

Doodle teddy to life . . . add buttons,
patches, snaps, zippers, etc.

A: BECAUSE LAUGHTER IS THE BEST MEDICINE.

Finish the joke!

A: JUST PUT IT ON MY BILL!

Doodle the duck and what it is quacking.

A: FROST BITE.

Doodle a frightened snowman.

A: THEY DON'T LIKE TO BE SPOTLESS.

Who's tugging the doggie?

Q: WHAT DOES A RABBIT USE TO FIX ITS FUR?

A: HARE SPRAY.

Doodle the rabbit's mirror image.

Q: WHAT DO YOU CALL A BOOMERANG
   THAT DOES NOT COME BACK?

A: A STICK.

Draw the devastated child.

Q: WHY WAS THE JELLY SO STRESSED OUT?

A: IT WAS SPREAD TOO THIN.

Doodle the joke. Who's in a jam? Bread? Knife?

Q: WHAT IS BLACK AND WHITE AND
   LAUGHING?

A: THE ZEBRA THAT PUSHED THE OTHER
   ZEBRA INTO THE SWIMMING POOL.

Where's the pushing zebra?
Add more things in the pool please!

Q: WHAT WAS THE ELEPHANT DOING ON
   THE FREEWAY?

A: I DON'T KNOW—ABOUT 10 MILES AN HOUR.

Doodle a big-headed elephant with ears
and trunk blowing in the wind.

Q: WHAT IS THE LARGEST ANT?

A: THE GI–ANT.

Finish the giant on each page and the background too.

Q: WHAT DID THE TRUMPETER SAY TO THE DRUMMER?

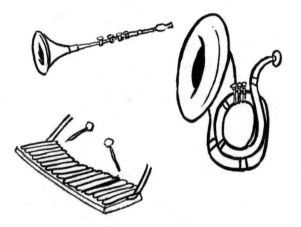

Who or what is in the marching band?

Q: WHAT IS THE MOST DIFFICULT TREE TO CLIMB AT SCHOOL?

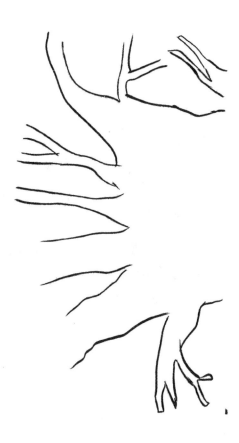

A: GEOMETRY!

Doodle what's on the tree . . . fruit, nuts, etc.
Is someone lying under the tree? Are there animals?

Q: WHERE DOES A DOG GO FOR ENTERTAINMENT?

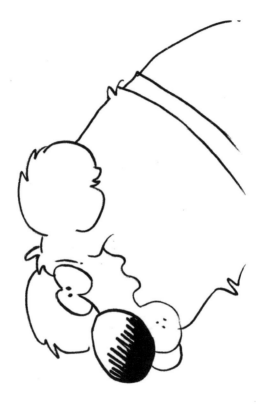

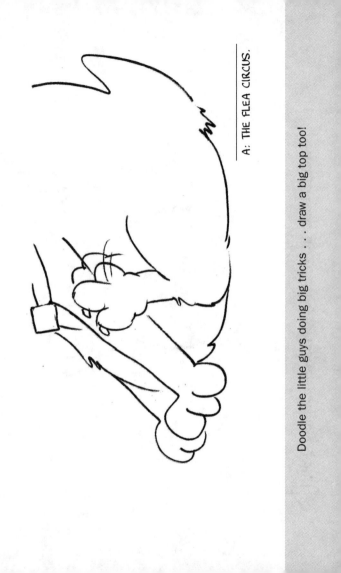

A: THE FLEA CIRCUS.

Doodle the little guys doing big tricks . . . draw a big top too!

Q: WHAT DOES A SNOWMAN USE FOR DIRECTIONS?

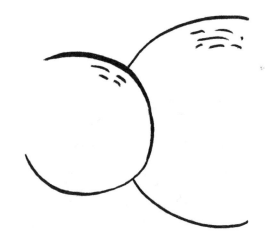

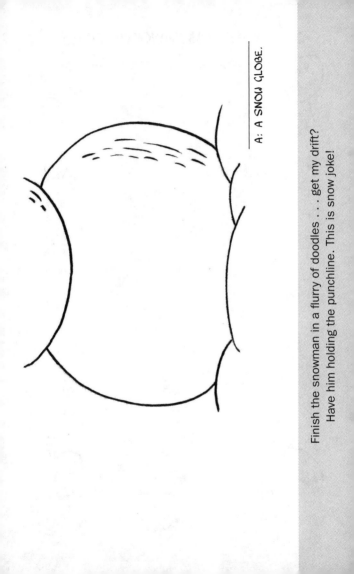

A: A SNOW GLOBE.

Finish the snowman in a flurry of doodles . . . get my drift?
Have him holding the punchline. This is snow joke!

Q: WHAT IS YOUR FAVORITE JOKE?

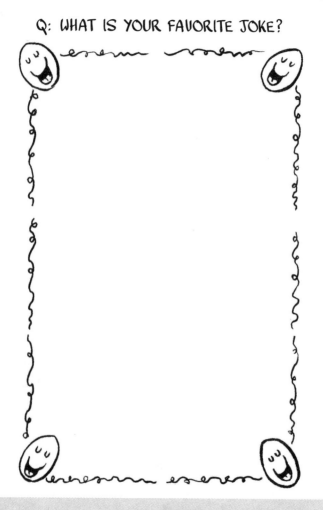

Write and draw it.

Q: EVER DRAW A BLANK? WE HAVE.

Fill it in with your humor and finish the book!

About the Author

Rob Elliott is the author of *Laugh-Out-Loud Jokes for Kids*, *More Laugh-Out-Loud Jokes for Kids*, *Laugh-Out-Loud Animal Jokes for Kids*, and *Knock-Knock Jokes for Kids*, and has been a publishing professional for more than twenty years. Rob lives in **West Michigan**, where in his spare time he enjoys laughing out loud with his wife and five children.

About the Illustrator

Jonny Hawkins is a full-time cartoonist whose work has appeared in over six hundred publications, including *Reader's Digest*, *Parade Magazine*, *The Saturday Evening Post*, and *Guideposts*. His illustrations have appeared in many books including the Chicken Soup for the Soul series, and he has created forty-eight successful page-a-day cartoon calendars (over 400,000 sold). He works from his home in **Sherwood, Michigan**, where he lives with his wife, Carissa, and their three children, four cats, and a dog.

The original.
The classic.
Destined to be America's favorite joke book.

Knock knock.
Who's there?
Ben.
Ben who?
Ben away for a while but I'm back now.

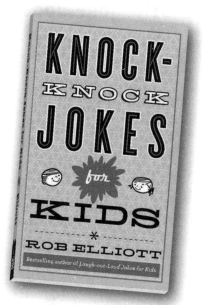

Don't miss Rob Elliott's bestselling book
of knock-knock jokes.

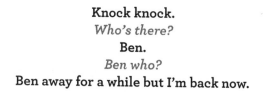

NEW from Popular Joke Book Author
Rob Elliott

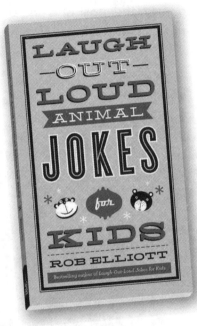

This collection of animal-themed jokes
is perfect for animal lovers and young
comedians everywhere.

Revell
a division of Baker Publishing Group
www.RevellBooks.com

DADS AND DAUGHTERS HAVE A SPECIAL RELATIONSHIP.

Let Rob and Joanna Teigen show you how to make the most of it and build memories that will last a lifetime.

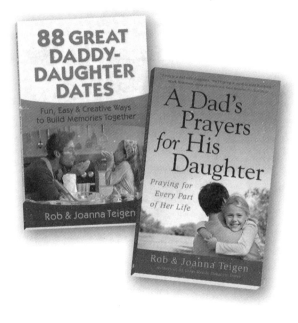